# Contents

| | |
|---|---|
| Preface | v |
| Chapter I: Who Are the Career Assistants? | 1 |
| Chapter II: The Portrait | 7 |
| Chapter III: How Programs and Policies Affect the Career Assistant Principal | 37 |
| Appendix A: Research Methods | 51 |
| Appendix B: Focus Group Interview Guide | 55 |
| Appendix C: Open-Ended Survey | 57 |
| References | 61 |

# The Unsung Role of the Career Assistant Principal

**By Catherine Marshall**
Professor of Educational Leadership
University of North Carolina-Chapel Hill

National Association of
Secondary School Principals
1904 Association Dr.,
Reston, Va. 22091-1537
(703) 860-0200

ABOUT THE AUTHOR: Catherine Marshall, a former teacher, is a professor in the Department of Educational Leadership at the University of North Carolina, Chapel Hill.

ISBN 0-88210-272-9

Copyright 1993
National Association of Secondary School Principals
1904 Association Drive
Reston, Virginia 22091-1537
(703) 860-0200

Timothy J. Dyer, *Executive Director*
Maryellen Parker, *Director of Assistant Principal Services*
Robert V. Mahaffey, *Director of Publications and Marketing*
Carol A. Bruce, *Associate Director of Publications*

# Preface

Pay attention to the contributions of the career assistant principal. Identify the satisfaction, support, programs, and policies that make their work manageable. Take note of the values they assert in their work and in their personal lives. There are lessons to be found there.

These men and women care about young people and contribute to maintaining stability in schools and in youngsters' lives. They also provide an alternative model for educators who are trying to decide whether to make the family and life sacrifices required to move into higher visibility and higher status positions. Read, see the patterns in their lives, ponder their words, and learn.

This book is a descriptive report from research into the lives of 50 career assistant principals. It originated from conversations with members of the NASSP Committee on the Assistant Principalship who, with the thoughtful and careful guidance of Maryellen Parker, NASSP's Director of Assistant Principal Services, decided on this focus in the fall of 1991.

I owe special thanks to Parker and the Committee for their support and cooperation. Also, I am indebted to Jeanne Rogge Steele who, as research assistant, spent time in schools gathering data, and lent her analytic and journalistic skills to assist in writing an enticing, readable, and authentic research report. Most of all, I am indebted to those assistant principals who, through letters, phone calls, and conversations, guided us to those who are truly career assistants; and to those who gave their time and opened up their lives for interviews, shadowing, and surveys.

The study, and this report, differ from most research. Instead of compiling statistics, we have built a portrait. It is undergirded by the theory and related documentation already compiled in *The Assistant Principal: Leadership Choices and Challenges* (Marshall, 1992). Rather than providing prescriptions, this portrait invites you, the reader, to "get inside" the lives of career assistants. It invites you to follow them through their daily routines, to listen to their words and try to understand the values and priorities that guide them, and then to extract from that rich complexity some thoughtful insights and directions.

—C.M.

# Chapter I
# Who Are the Career Assistants?

## Facing and Defying the Stereotypes

> **gargoyle:** *A grotesque waterspout, made to resemble a human or animal figure with its mouth wide open, projecting from the gutter of a building (especially in Gothic architecture) in order to carry the rain water clear of the walls. The figures were part animal and part human. The largest ones extended as much as three feet from the walls of the building.*

The educational equivalent? The assistant principal, or so some people say. Others fall back on equally unflattering stereotypes: "chauvinist moron," "Reichsfuhrer," "Marine Corps sergeant type," or "Keystone Kop." These are the ways the mass media, parents, and sometimes even colleagues still view the assistant principalship, and that doesn't make those who serve in the position feel very good.

"Look at the media," said one assistant principal who was honored in 1992 as the best in his state. "When was the last time you saw a movie where the assistant principal was shown to be anything but a chauvinist moron who walks around with the big stick?"

Said another honoree, "Any time I mention that I'm an assistant principal to people, they say, 'Oh, discipline.' That's the only thing they associate with assistant principals. . . . We're the bad guys."

And, these professionals admit among themselves, such views are not surprising given the role of the assistant principal two and three decades ago, when many of today's parents were students. In those days, the assistant principal was often the "hammer guy," the former coach who walked down the hall screaming "get into the classroom." Worse, even today the person who stays in this position too often is viewed as a fool or a failure.

This research report defies such stereotypes. To be sure, there are still some "traditional, long-term assistant principals" around—the "good ole boys," as they are referred to by colleagues—who remain in their positions because no one is willing to rock the boat far enough to capsize it.

Far more prevalent, however, is a new breed of career assistants whose roles are as diverse as the students they serve. These career assistants view each day as a challenge.

"My job no longer deals strictly with discipline and attendance," one assistant explains. "I'm more involved with departments. I'm more involved with supervision. More involved as a counselor. More involved as, I hope, a trusted colleague of these people who come down and say I need some advice."

Who is this new breed of assistant principal? Certainly not a low achiever who remains in the administrative career for want of other options. That unstated but widely held stereotype is not supported by this research. On the contrary, this report documents rich and varied contributions made by these experienced educators who derive special personal and professional satisfactions from their stable positions.

## Why Study the Career Assistant Principal?

Although it does defy the stereotype, the main purpose of this study is to explore a two-part question: What motivates the person who is comfortable staying in the assistant principalship? And, how do these career assistant principals (APs) find support and make meaning of their lives and their work?

### A Teasing View of the Findings

The complete report provides a full display of answers to these questions. However, two summarizing findings are important: Career APs find rewards in working with children; and they set a high priority on maintaining healthy and balanced personal lives.

The most driving reward of career APs is the knowledge that they help young people grow and develop. Often, they stay in their positions in order to maintain balanced and stable personal lives. They find ways to use their discretion and flexibility to instill meaning in their work lives. At the same time, they sort out the rules and realities of school life. All educators can gain insights from examining the career and life choices as well as the philosophies and work interactions of these career APs.

For example, Chester Randall's work day begins as he selects a wild tie and a far-out hat from his attention-getting collection. As the buses roll in and he banters with the middle school students, he explains, "It gives them some handle to talk with me and laugh with me; at least they have one way of connecting with an adult that day."

Career APs devise an array of tactics for molding and shaping the school setting and its many points of people-contact so that the students, teachers, custodians and cafeteria workers, and parents and community members keep on believing in the school's meaning and purpose.

At the same time, these assistant principals sort through their own life purposes and decide that they value the balanced and controllable work and personal life derived from staying put where they are.

"At age 40 I made a decision that my whole life wasn't going to be school," said Randall, as he described how he came to accept and enjoy being a career AP.

A new wife, a circle of good friends, the chance to go out socially two or three times a week, were pleasurable and realizing alternatives to the pressures of upward mobility in the administrative career. He came to the realization that the stresses of a recent divorce, a family history of heart disease, and the fact that long ago he'd earned a reputation for being outspoken, were all reasons to stay put until retirement.

Others explain staying put in the assistant principalship by stressing their decisions to enjoy their family life, or their desire to avoid the visibility, stresses, and "politics" of higher positions.

The hierarchy of the administrative career (and the salary, power, and status that accompany it) builds in assumptions that energetic and motivated educators should try to move up the ladder. Career assistants, however, put their energies into their current positions. Like Randall, most have an array of professional and personal reasons that, put together, make their career choice a very sane and healthy one.

Their reasons provide useful insights for those who would support their work (e.g., professional associations, school boards and central office personnel, and principals). In addition, for those who wonder about how to manage the stresses and ensure the health and well-being of administrators, and for those who worry about how to recruit and support educational leaders, these career APs provide an alternate way of viewing the administrative career.

Unlike those who are enmeshed in the struggle to the top, many career APs have found a challenging career in educational administration that allows them an opportunity for creativity, some freedom, and a reasonable chance to have a stable and well-rounded family life. As important, career APs and their colleagues know their work is crucial to school stability; they know their contribution goes far beyond the 30-some tasks they accomplish on any given day to include a deep-rooted caring for students and skill at making important connections among adults in schools.

*Theory and Research Questions*

This study is based on the theory that people make career choices after sorting through a complex set of considerations about themselves as persons and comparing those values and realities with a range of signals, norms, requirements, and realities in the environment of their career. That theory, then, guided the framing of these questions:

- What is the career assistant principalship like?
- What makes people consider keeping the job?
- How do they make the job meaningful, in the long run?
- What is special about those who keep the job?
- What is special about their career environment?
- What policies, structures, and programs support them?
- What helpful hints can be gleaned from their careers?

*Insights from Previous Research*

In the past, a majority of assistant principals viewed their positions as temporary stepping stones from which to launch themselves into higher positions (Austin and Brown, 1970). More recently, intensive case studies explored how assistants develop their orientation to the career (Marshall, 1992; Marshall et. al., 1991). Many earn the label "upwardly mobile" as they set their sights on quick movement to principalships and higher. Others, after encountering important changes in district priorities, losing their sponsor, or taking risks or political stands that cause career trouble, may be labeled as "shafted;" they cannot move up and they are angry. Others are "plateaued" as they continue to search for new positions with decreasing opportunity to move.

Still others are "downwardly mobile," likely to move back to the teaching ranks or lower-prestige positions, often because of reductions in force or rule changes. Those who are "considering leaving" have interesting career options outside education and are finding the assistant principalship less and less interesting. Finally, the career AP is the person who finds satisfaction in the assistant principalship and will probably stay in the position until retirement.

The focus of this study is the career assistant principal. Because schools are structured so that the powerful motivators of power, money, and status come to those who move higher and higher up the ladder, why are these people reasonably content in their positions?

## What and Who Is in This Study?

Diving into the real school setting is the only way to understand the interplay among career APs, their career environments, their daily tasks and roles, and their idiosyncratic approaches to meaning-making. This study represents an invigorating plunge into that world. A more complete description of the research methods and the range of sites and the sample is included in Appendix A.

Briefly, two researchers observed and shadowed 10 assistants, interviewed them, their principals, spouses, colleagues, and others who had observed their work over a long term. In addition, focus group interviewing (of 14 award-winning APs) and surveys (of 26 APs) were used to gain a wider perspective and to verify the findings from the more intensive observation and interviewing.

Respondents came from nearly half the states, and from urban, rural, and suburban districts. The respondents ranged from assistants with a few years' experience to one with 23 years in the same position. They were in elementary, middle, and high schools, with varied demographic and economic situations. School sizes ranged from enrollments of 500 to 1,800; schools had one to three assistant principals.

The findings emerged in the form of patterns that were prevalent across the data on career APs. Data analysis was guided by career socialization theory and by a range of related research about the administrative career. Rich and deeply contextual data were collected, including documents (e.g., job descriptions and schedules), pages of field observations (e.g., observations of office arrangements; parking lot, cafeteria, and corridor conversations), and notes detailing the steady stream of people interactions that characterize a career AP's work day, plus transcripts from hours of taped interview.

The report that follows is a presentation of the patterns that become clear from examining the data. It is written so that, as much as possible, that rich context is displayed and career APs tell their own story with illustrative quotes. Where the respondents are identified, pseudonyms are used.

Section I of the report sets up the assumptions and premises of the study. Section II describes the work and the people in rich detail. Section III identifies patterns by focusing on the career environment. Policies, programs, and structural supports that assist the career AP are identified.

# Chapter II
# The Portrait

*And I will firmly believe until the day I die that that has been my calling to deal with young people and to relate to them.*

*I don't really have a bad day. . . . It's hard for me to have a bad day unless somebody comes in here with a gun.*

By presenting detailed descriptions of the settings, the tasks, and the people interactions that fill each day to overflowing, this section presents a portrait of career APs. It embellishes the portrait with earthy and representative quotes revealing the rewards and the values of career APs, thus framing the portrait for use in both long-term decision making and day-to-day interactions. No demographic tables or compilations of statistics are presented; rather, an authentic, useful, and evocative picture is drawn.

From the portrait, policymakers, staff developers, and educators can pull implications for policy, programs, and career decision making. The portrait begins with the background—the setting and tasks that frame the career AP's work, but immediately adds nuances of meaning by providing details and quotes.

## The Setting

Career APs are among the first people to arrive at school in the morning, and most often they hit the ground running. Frequently, their first stop is at the front desk to pick up discipline notices from the preceding day. Then it's a quick pass through detention hall, just to let students there know that compliance with school regulations is both noted and appreciated.

Next may come a quick cup of coffee with the principal or some teachers, a before-school conference with parents who need to get to work, or a sneak attack on the inevitable pile of paperwork that threatens to take over the desk top. Once students begin to arrive, the career AP starts walking.

"Where else," asked one woman career AP, "would you get paid for walking miles?"

School corridors, formal banquet halls, and conference rooms; football stadiums, auditoriums, cafeterias; parking lots and gymnasiums—wherever the center of activity is—that's where you'll find the career AP. The work setting can expand into the woods through which youngsters walk to and from school, and it can include the police station when a student gets into trouble. It extends as far as the school's reach. In fact, it incorporates the entire community.

### The Office

"If no one knows where to send someone or what to do with something, it ends up in my office. I mean no matter what it is. It really does."

The door is usually open and the desk faces out; there's always a place to talk. Career APs' offices are public places. Their ornamentation and the steady stream of people coming and going demonstrate that career APs are people-persons, whose job is the serious monitoring of adherence to the school mission. Posters with anti-drug messages or plaques recognizing professional achievement might be on the walls, and professional journals, policy manuals, and books about education are sure to be on the bookshelves.

File cabinets and desk drawers are filled with inventories of books and materials, staff evaluations, student records, and scheduling grids. Some APs use computers for scheduling and student records. These desktop processors and the walkie-talkies many career APs carry as they rove the buildings and grounds are the main technological advances in the work of the career assistant principal.

Typically, the career AP's office is sparsely furnished and unpretentious. One has to be alert for clues that provide insights into who these people are as individuals. In one office, a collection of beautiful glass apples attests to a special relationship between the career AP and her principal. In another, a little wooden top opens the door to stories about the career AP's avocation as a flea-market antique dealer. A box full of walnut scrapwood in a third office leads to the discovery that the owner is a skilled woodworker whose handcrafted pipes are highly sought after.

In every case, it is people—students, primarily—who make the career AP's office come alive. The chances of finding a career AP alone in his or her office are slim.

One career AP advises, "Close your door—that's the only way to keep the job manageable." But the doors are seldom closed.

Even the contents of desk drawers offer revealing insights.

"I think convenience stores were created just to keep us busy," Chester Randall, a middle school career AP, remarked as he opened a desk drawer full of squirt guns, firecrackers, chewing gum, plastic vomit and novelty store dog poop, pornographic cards, and handcuffs collected over the years.

## The Cafeteria and Corridors

"I see a lot of good things going on in the building. Being able to talk with the teachers, just picking up on the little things and letting teachers know. . . . It makes them feel good, and it should. They're doing such wonderful things, they should feel good about it."

Outsiders forget the activity, noise, and heat generated during a lunch period—the one time during the day when one-third to one-half the student population converges into a relatively unstructured setting. Just getting the students through the cafeteria doors without incident is no small feat, particularly at the high school level, where already-adult bodies are charged with adolescent energy levels. APs monitor the cafeteria during lunch breaks, which are usually staggered over several periods in order to accommodate all the students. Sometimes, they are assisted by teachers assigned to cafeteria duty for one period a day.

The cafeteria setting can be volatile, but it can also be fun. Chester Randall and his fellow AP use the cafeteria as the setting for quick conversations with middle school students. They talk about the food, their T-shirts, yearbook pictures, or their fathers' golf games. The topic of conversation is not nearly as important as the connection.

At another school, a proudly "punk" teenager, dressed all in black and sporting the obligatory earrings, chain, and Roman cross of the heavy-metal set, checks in with career AP Michael Sullivan, who asks him about his new "do." The youth has shaved one side of his head clean, while preserving a mane of unkempt, once-black but now-blond tresses on the other side. The effect is eye-catching, to say the least.

"Some teachers are scared of him," Sullivan confides. "He says he's an atheist, and they're threatened by him. We have satanists, kids on drugs. . . . I just treat them like kids—fairly—and let them know what I expect. It seems to work."

Another somewhat-tough-looking young lady calls Sullivan over to her table, and he comes back laughing out loud. He explains that she wanted to know who the stranger was. Black himself, Sullivan said he replied, 'Oh, she's my white shadow.' She got quite a kick out of that, I guess."

And for the rest of the day, the researcher was introduced as Sullivan's "white shadow."

Such banter is characteristic of career APs as they set the tone for interaction in the cafeteria, knowing that the easy, personalized interactions help establish needed relationships between the adults and the youngsters in the schools.

On the other hand, trouble in the cafeteria is not unknown. Career APs believe half their job is "just being seen," so they spend most of their time standing in conspicuous places, keeping an eye on what's going on.

Sullivan explained that you get to know the patterns, who sits with whom, and which groups tend to keep a distance. When the pattern changes, "that's when you go on alert."

His associate AP, a woman, wound up on the cafeteria floor the previous week, he said, while trying to break up a fight between two "little" girls.

"Decker got them apart," he said, "but she ended up on her knees on the floor." (Imagining this well-dressed, professional-looking woman in the midst of a hair-pulling free-for-all goes a long way toward undoing any misconceptions about the AP position being boring.)

Barney Harris described how he had retained half the student body in the lunch room after a food fight. Following a lecture about how the "lunch ladies" had made good meals for them all year and the foot fight was an inappropriate response, he pointed them to the custodian's supply closet and said "go to it." No students were permitted to leave the cafeteria until they had used the cleaning supplies to full effect on every surface—chairs, tables, and floor—in the room.

At the elementary school level, fist fights and food fights are rarer, but the noise level is equally high. In this setting, the challenge is to wipe away the tears caused by spilled milk, to make sure that everyone has something to eat and someone to eat with, and to pretend the child-sized tables and chairs are something other than crippling for adults. The rewards for such diligence, at least in Marie Miller's school, are hug after hug from little ones encountered going and coming in the halls.

Whereas elementary school career APs love "walking the halls," school corridors are less beloved by middle level and secondary school administrators, who must constantly be on the lookout for young lovers whose hormones won't wait for school to be out or rebellious smokers who light up the minute they find a deserted staircase or unpatrolled corridor. Career APs pride themselves on knowing all the favorite hiding places. "It's almost like a game," Sullivan said, explaining that he likes to temper firmness with humor.

Days earlier, in keeping with that philosophy, he had borrowed a bike that had been left on the school grounds and rode it all around the campus—upstairs and down—through the corridors and around the open courtyard where students congregate on warm days. The kids got quite a chuckle out of his "mobile patrol."

The very same bike would soon be auctioned off, he explained, at a year-end auction for special education students. Throughout the year, these students are able to earn "chits" for good behavior. Come June, they can spend the "money" they have earned at the auction.

"In a few days, I'll go out and call upon some of the local businesses to see if they'll donate something for these kids," Sullivan said, acknowledging a role he takes on, not because it is assigned, but because he sees the positive benefits for kids. Earlier, he had described his philosophy of education this way: "They're [the students] our customers and we need to do everything we can to make their stay here exciting and challenging."

As can be seen, cafeterias and corridors are not static settings. Watching career APs make their rounds reveals the myriad ways they monitor the safety and stability of their schools. As important, they use every interaction (typically 8 to 10 per minute) as a chance to establish and maintain connections with students and the other adults in the school.

Sometimes the exchanges are trivial (e.g., asking for a bite of a student's cupcake); at other times, they couch important moral messages (e.g., ridiculing a boy about his excuses for getting into his second fight that day). Sometimes, career APs single out the prettier girls or the "jocks" for attention, or the child whose father is well-connected in the community. As often, they find a way to let an unpopular student know that at least one adult noticed him that day. In these small ways, career APs make connections, maintain stability, and make meaning of life in schools.

### The Grounds, Parking Lot, and Beyond

"She certainly makes a contribution all over, but I think I value her most as someone who can help in decision making. . . . She just kind of complements everything that I do. It really is a team approach."

Career APs have a mental map of their workplace. It extends far beyond the school grounds to an extended network of resources that can be used to prevent problems and circumvent threats to the stability of the school or even an individual student.

As he managed a meeting of specialists convened to decide how to manage one problem student, Fred Meece pulled from his years of experience in his community.

That this high school student had been in a violent fight with her boyfriend and was expelled just before final testing was only the immediate problem. Compounding it were these realities: she was a special education student; she was pregnant; she might or might not be living with her grandmother; and she could not be in the same building with her boyfriend without risk of another fight.

Meece knew all these things. He made judgments about where the girl was actually living, despite what the official school record showed, based on what he had observed her eating for breakfast. The labels on her take-out food were the telltale sign. Determined that she would at least get to take her final exams, Meece relied on his detailed knowledge of district facilities as he arranged for the teenager to take her finals at a nearby school, well away from the path of her ex-boyfriend.

Career APs go to work whenever there is a connection between students' lives and school-related activities. They garner useful information wherever they find it; from convenience store managers, fast food labels, cars arriving in the parking lot, calls from concerned parents or friends, or telltale circles under the eyes of students who work to support themselves. The signs are there for anyone to read, but frequently it takes a career AP to make sense of them.

Most career APs are fiercely protective of their schools and their students. Even though the skies overhead were as black as night and she was wearing heels and a stylish dress, Marie Miller didn't hesitate one minute when she spotted some older boys taking their time as they headed home from the middle school that is a parking lot and open field away from hers. She hiked right into the woods to ensure that her elementary students could walk home in peace, without interference from the older students.

It's not the exception but the rule for career APs to anticipate potential dangers or complications. They are the ones to make sure that students and parents have explicit directions for getting to banquets, basketball play-offs, and spring proms. They carefully cultivate long-term relationships with social service agencies, police, business sponsors, health care providers, and a range of other professionals who can assist them.

The school's driveway is the twice daily setting for "bus duty." The career AP's knowledge of students' lives is greatly enhanced as they monitor safe entrance and exit from schools.

Edward Stovall noted, "I truly enjoy the bus drivers; they know more about where our students come from than any highly trained school psychologist or counselor. They see it every day." He went on to describe how he carefully establishes good relations with these unrecognized child development experts who can manage buses and young people at the same time.

## The Whole Community

Unlike some professionals who can shut their office doors and leave work behind, career APs are still on the job when they're doing their grocery shopping, enjoying a game of golf, or walking up the steps to church on Sunday. The work setting spills over into the community for at least three reasons: choice, longevity, and school and community expectations. Some career APs love the visibility; others could do without it. But they all seem to adapt in one way or another.

Mary Alice Kincaid loves teenagers and she loves being with people. At 63, she has been in education for more than 30 years, and she isn't about to retire just yet.

Whereas her principal confesses to being anti-social after school hours, Kincaid and her husband divide their "free" time between school events and social functions connected to his work. For them, going to science fairs; basketball and football games; volleyball, wrestling, and tennis matches; school dances and pep rallies is fun, not work.

Mr. Kincaid goes, "primarily to be with her," but he admits to having a ball when he's around young people. In fact, he suspects that even when he and Mary Alice are both retired, they will continue to go to school functions simply because they enjoy it. A firm believer in positive motivation, he thinks that teenagers deserve to hear that "they've done well . . . because that constant reinforcement is so much more important than anything else."

Clearly proud of his wife's accomplishments, Kincaid says parents are always stopping her in the shopping center or at the mall to tell her how their sons or daughters or, more frequently now, even their grandchildren are doing. It doesn't matter whether they're physicians or plumbers, he says, "she rejoices in their success, no matter what they may do."

For one career AP who is single and female, visibility in the community means resisting the temptation to run out to the mailbox in "something you're real comfortable in because somebody's going to say, 'I saw you at your mailbox.'" She finds the visibility of the position both good and bad. "Bad because you are on display; but good because they know you as a person who does have to grocery shop, who does have to go to the drycleaner. Good in that they feel comfortable coming up and saying, 'How are you doing?' Or, 'I haven't seen you out. . . .'"

For another, being an AP in a town of about 16,000 people for 17 years has resulted in his becoming the town father, of sorts. Whether he's on the golf course or out running with a friend, it's not unusual for his companion to ask for advice about how to handle this or that situation. About the same age as many of the parents, he has become "like a personal coach to them now that their kids are coming through the school."

In larger high schools, knowing a lot of faces can sometimes be a liability. One AP shared a funny story about "when the career AP goes shopping." As he tells it, the career AP walks innocently down the aisle at the supermarket, his wife by his side, and they encounter a young lady who looks familiar to him.

"And she looks at you like 'Don't I know you?'"

So knowing how sensitive former students are when their career AP fails to greet them, he offers a friendly, "Hi," only to get a "what's-that-dirty-old-man-looking-at" look in response.

Career APs are also asked to serve on community boards and commissions. School or youth-related organizations such as the Special Olympics, Little League, 4-H, Boy Scouts, and Girl Scouts welcome their involvement, as do civic organizations like Rotary, Kiwanis, and the Lions Club. Career APs especially are sought after, one said, because "some of the best people you can have in your organization are assistant principals. They know you're going to get the job done."

Some career APs thrive on such involvements: their work, community visibility, and leisure activities flow together. Admittedly a workaholic, Fred Meece is proud to be a Lion and enjoys socializing with other Lions.

"I had other opportunities and didn't want to move," he said. "I love the town. . . ."

Another AP, who lives and works in a small farming community, said, "In a small community, you get to know a lot of people. You go out to dinner, or you go out for a beer with the guys after a ball game or something, and everybody's talking to you. That personal relationship is unbelievable."

Others, however, steer clear. Once active in Little League and Legion baseball, one veteran and award-winning AP curtailed his activities with youngsters when he became an assistant principal. His reason: to get away from doing the same thing all over again.

Being highly visible provides status and self-worth. However, as Barney Harris found, it leaves the career AP vulnerable when students vent frustrations. "I'm sure it was kids I'd disciplined, but I know I was doing right to give them tough guidance," he said, explaining his reaction to his house being spray painted.

Although career APs are ambivalent about their roles as mentors, community leaders, and preservers of community standards, their elevated stature—whether deserved or desired—dates back to the earliest days of public education in this country, when being a teacher was one of the most revered professions in town.

Although times have certainly changed since the days when the young "school mistress" had to live in a private home, take her meals with the family, and turn her light out by 10 o'clock, many people—superintendents, school board members, and principals included—still value the contribution career APs make to town-gown relations.

Commenting on Michael Sullivan's value to his high school, Principal Stan Lilley said, "If he were to retire, I could never replace him." For one thing, Sullivan is black, and Lilley believes it's tremendously important to have minorities represented in administration.

But even more important, Lilley said, "He's a local person. He lives here in the community, and he serves as a role model as well as a reality check. He can't be conned very easily because he knows kids and he knows their families. He knows when they're shooting him a line."

It alarms Lilley, he said, that he doesn't "see a lot of Michael Sullivans coming along." Principal of a high school in a largely rural district that is slowly being swallowed up as a bedroom community by larger cities on both sides, Lilley says there are fewer minority administrators coming up through the ranks, and those who are "tend to live in large cities."

"I might," he says, "and that's a *big* [his emphasis] might . . . be able to find another minority administrator. But I can guarantee you that I can't find one who lives in this community, goes to church here, and shops at the local grocery stores."

Connections with the heart of the community provide valuable understanding and legitimacy for any school administrator. "Parents have a nice warm feeling about the school when they see him," Sullivan's counterpart AP affirmed. "He brings a continuity to the position that no one else has. He's been a tremendous resource in knowing how the community will react. And his knowledge of individual families—knowing the name of a cousin, a brother, a parent, the place where someone works—has been a tremendous help to me."

From this rich description, one can see the intertwining of the work setting with the tasks and roles, values and philosophies of the career AP. The next section focuses more specifically on tasks, but once again they must be understood within the context of deeper meanings.

## Tasks and Roles

"Some people say assistant principals do what the principals don't want to do, and maybe that's the true description of it."

Some career APs have formal job descriptions that include headings such as bus supervision, book orders, equipment inventory, building maintenance, scheduling, and substitute teachers. Responsibility for a portion of teacher evaluations and cocurricular activities are usually incorporated. Other assignments include community school scheduling, parking supervision, and staff development.

Discipline usually appears somewhere, with responsibility frequently being apportioned by grade level. Such assignments are made on the basis of individual propensity and skill, district tradition, and need.

"The best thing the principal does for an assistant is to define the job and then let him do it without petty interference," said one seasoned educator, a 56-year-old who, as teacher and AP, has worked with 10 principals.

However, other career APs have no job descriptions at all. In their view, the position is simply "not describable." Even career APs who like the certainty of clearly stated expectations are well aware that written descriptions are bland statements that never can capture the full range and meaning of what they do.

Tomes, not mere statements, would be required to describe the unwritten tasks and roles of the career AP, who, depending on the hour and the day, may serve as confidant or sounding board to the principal; marriage counselor or shoulder to cry on for a colleague in crisis; smoke bomb dismantler, gun detector, or underground drug agent. Some roles are thrust upon the career AP without warning; other projects, programs, and tasks are carved out and jealously guarded by the individual who has chosen to make a career of the assistant principalship.

Valued by some principals and merely tolerated by others, the career AP almost always brings stability and breadth of experience to the position. Invariably loyal to their schools and protective of their students, career APs are characterized not just by a willingness but rather an ingrained commitment to "making things work."

One principal, of one of these special people, described his career AP this way: "I think he's always been the kind of person who just felt that what he does is important—whether as a teacher or as an administrator—and that there were people out there depending on him and that he needed to deliver."

In other words, career APs want to help. How they translate that idealism into their day-to-day routines depends on any number of factors, not the least of which is what's happening each day.

## The Diversity

"Assistant principals have to have some kind of kid contact. You can teach a wonderful seminar to faculty, or you can work with support services and at-risk teenagers. But when you notch your gunbelt, it's 'I think I helped this kid, or I think I helped that kid.'"

For career APs in charge of substitute teachers, things start happening as early as 5:30 in the morning. That's when teachers who have been up all night with the flu or with sick children call to inform the school that they can't make it to work that day.

That's also the time when administrators in New England and the upper midwest decide whether it's safe to let the school buses roll. If it's a "snow day," both radio stations and bus drivers must be called well before sunrise.

Sometimes, it's a custodian on the other end of the line, calling to let the career AP in charge of maintenance know there's no heat in the building, or that the air-cooling system is out thanks to overnight storms.

In some smaller school districts, the career AP may hear directly from a bus driver who, for whatever the reason, can neither drive that day nor find a substitute licensed to drive a school bus. Then, it's a quick shower, maybe a cup of coffee, throw on some clothes, jump into the car, and drive to wherever the bus is parked.

A combination of fast reflexes, alert children, and maybe a little prayer help to keep such versatile career APs on the right route.

Some career APs start their day by giving the public address announcements; others have a cup of coffee with their principal and discuss "what happened yesterday and what's going on today." Although no two days are alike, there is a rhythm or pattern to the way career APs structure their time. And people notice when these patterns change.

A focus group participant illustrated the problem this way: "I give the announcements and set the tone, but for some reason my principal gave the announcements the other day and something didn't work. I'm concrete and sequential; he's not. And within five minutes a teacher came in and said, 'Oh my, that was a principal announcement. Things are just falling apart out here.'"

Although he didn't realize it until it was too late, this career AP typically had a plan going before he picked up the microphone. Without that kind of forethought, the school day got off to a rocky start.

When the bell signals second period, Michael Sullivan reports to the cafeteria, where he meets with his assigned homeroom students. The day we shadowed him, he had brought graduation cards for the kids to sign—a homeroom remembrance (no doubt paid for out of his own pocket) for the two seniors who would graduate the following Sunday.

A year-long, school spirit, team building experiment initiated by the principal, Sullivan's homeroom had to meet in the cafeteria because his office was too small to accommodate the dozen or so students drawn from all four class levels. Even though he spent just 10 minutes with them each day in a cavernous room where it is impossible to hear anything below a shout, Sullivan clearly knew each student by name, temperament, academic program, and special need.

As the school day progresses, career APs tackle a multitude of tasks. They range from evaluating a teacher to investigating a minor bus accident, from processing book orders to celebrating a birthday, from ushering a timid new student to her classroom to delivering keys to a new custodian.

And always there is discipline and caring for youngsters. The former can be scheduled or unscheduled.

On days when one of Mary Alice Kincaid's assistants are on hand (students work with her in conjunction with a cooperative education program), they make the rounds of classrooms and bring students charged with breaking school rules to her office. When she doesn't have help, she makes up a "little list and I just go down the halls and see which ones I'm supposed to see. And that's quicker sometimes."

A former guidance counselor, Kincaid says that as an AP, "you probably do more counseling than you do in a guidance office."

Many of her colleagues would agree. In the group discussion, one said, "I don't have a counseling background. I never did. But I feel that probably half of what I do when I'm dealing with kids is counseling, and my eyes were never opened so wide as in the first year as assistant principal. I taught school for 14 years, but I didn't see the depth of problems that my students had until I sat at the assistant principal's desk."

Another discussed how she had worked as a volunteer mediator, and the training she received gave her more tools for her job than any other experience. "It's wonderful, because that's what a lot of parents need when they come in with their kids. I do a mediation right there."

A great deal of a career AP's time is spent teaching parenting skills and dealing with the effects of outside influences. Suicide threats, sexual abuse, pregnancies, drugs, guns—all the problems that make headlines eventually end up with the career AP.

"We spend more time with people's kids than they spend with them themselves," remarked a member of one focus group. Others agreed that even the best of parents are grateful for career APs simply being there.

"We're there with their kids all the time, even when they can't be there because of job, other kids, work, school, whatever. But we're there."

The amount of time career APs physically spend "on the job" is not to be taken lightly. APs in one district kept track and found out they were putting in an average of 71 hours per week. Because career APs are in the building more than almost any other staff members, people tend to turn to them first—no matter what the problem.

"The fact is that when the need arises, it's most often the AP who's there," said one woman. "And whether it's a kid or a staff member, they know when you're gone," chimed in another colleague.

"'Where were you?' they'll ask, and the rest of that is simply understood . . . 'because I needed you,' or 'I needed to have this information,' or . . . ."

Career APs know that they frequently have a much broader base of information about what is going on in their schools than their principals, because of "all those bits and pieces of information coming in."

Their intimate knowledge of their schools and the tremendous amount of time they spend at the school site affect the roles career APs play. "I've been in the business long enough now that there are few surprises. I short-circuit problems because I know what to expect," relates one veteran.

Other career APs attest to serving as a kind of "buffer" or "filter" for their principals. "My goal is to try to solve as many problems as possible before they get through to him," Chester Randall explained.

One discussant suggested that even the task of training new principals falls to the career AP. Noting that new principals are sometimes assigned to schools with which they have no experience (e.g., a middle school AP is appointed principal of an elementary school), he said, "So it all comes down to you anyway, as to how you do this or what the procedures are for that. And you end up training your principal as well as other new staff members."

Listening is another important aspect of the career AP's job—listening to people who are angry, sad, stressed out, or simply perplexed. "Many a time," said one career AP, "I am almost a safety valve to parents, students, and teachers, because when teachers are having a problem, they'll come into my office and just vent. Perhaps not to ask for advice as much as to just vent. It's just the idea that they have a place that they can feel is a safe haven."

Another career AP told about a long-time department coordinator who, after an informal conversation over a cup of coffee, said, "George, you're the first guy that's really listened to me."

The storyteller continued, "You know, he said that and two days later another one said that, and that's why what we've been talking about has meant so much to me—because this sensitivity thing is so important to me. I believe in that."

"Trust" is another word that frequently comes up when career APs seek to define their roles. One man described the satisfaction he gets when a youngster comes into his office and says, "I have to talk with you. I have this problem with these kids, or I don't know what to do with this teacher."

Sometimes the problem is not so simple, however. For instance, a student comes in and it is clear the youngster is troubled about something. "I just say, 'Have a seat. You want to talk about it?' And the student says, 'You know, don't you?' And I say, 'Yes. What are you going to do?' That kind of thing. But I think it's the trust factor; assistant principals probably have the most trust in an entire building."

Supporting the work of teachers is another role many career APs take on. One focus group participant said that one of the things she found most rewarding about her job was doing teacher evaluations. "They're formative," she said, adding, "I'm about the business of watching teachers who are doing a good job, and helping them build on what they're doing . . . ."

Fred Meece described himself as the "cheer person" who organizes coffee hours, staff outings, and socials at his school. "Our staff is so large," he said, "that we'd never see each other without such coffee and doughnut times."

Marie Miller dedicated an entire year to helping an inexperienced teacher, who had received a bad evaluation after her first year, develop the self-confidence and classroom skills she would need to continue in the teaching profession.

By combining skills training, coaching, and an ample measure of encouragement, Miller, with 22 years of teaching experience to guide her, turned what could have been a failing teacher into a promising one.

Minority career APs carve out their own special roles and respond to a difference set of school and student needs. For years, one career AP filled the role of "token black" at schools where he was the only minority administrator.

Another black man said he enjoyed trying to inspire youngsters. "I like to serve as a role model for them and show them they can do things themselves. I do a little Black History at some of these [area] schools, and give demonstrations on how I do that."

We found that almost without exception, career APs dress well, comport themselves with grace, and treat students politely and respectfully. They expect the same in return.

Interwoven with all these roles is discipline, the one task that most career APs just can't get away from. Some thrive on it. Others see it as a burden. As one career AP put it, "Any time I mention I'm an assistant principal to other people, they say, 'Oh, discipline.' That's the only thing they associate with assistant principal. They don't realize that we work on curriculum committees, that we evaluate teachers, that we're working on staff development, and all the other things that we do.

"I'm proud that we can do that job [of discipline] because it has to be done. But all these other things are important, too, and if you only did the one and didn't have your hand in these other things, then I think it would be a terrible job."

Michael Sullivan is philosophical about discipline. To some people, he says, discipline is love. To others, it is punishment. For him, it is teaching behavior. "I consider everything I do instructional," he explained. "Where we fall short is trying to separate discipline from instruction. I think we need a new word for discipline."

Marie Miller handles discipline quietly. The secretary at her school said, "She handles it so well that sometimes we don't even know a child has been brought back there—that she's disciplined them and moved them back out to class."

Career assistants who have been in their positions for many years, particularly at one school, end up with cumulative responsibilities. One focus group participant, who had been at the same school for 23 years, explained it this way: "And even though your role changes and your job duties change, you know what happens? They still call you, and you don't say, 'Oh, you've got to call so-and-so now.' No, you go ahead and deal with it."

### Carving Out the Position

"The way I view the role of the assistant principal, or the way I choose to carry it out, gives me more choice. I don't have to be in the limelight all the time like the principal. So I have the choice to have time with my family away from school. People know that those are my values, and as an assistant principal they can accommodate them more."

The roles and tasks that a career AP takes on—or, perhaps more accurately, the way those roles and tasks are carried out—depend greatly on two additional factors: the individual's temperament and attitude toward his or her work, and how well the administrative team functions together as a unit. When there's a good fit, career APs rhapsodize about the team relationships with their principal and fellow APs.

But the job can be miserable when trust dissipates, or when administrators cannot communicate well. Almost uniformly, career APs attribute success or failure on the communications front to the principal.

Said one: "I think the key is that relationship with your principal. Where do your values and views of leadership and the leadership role either meld together or come into conflict? That's the person who makes the real decisions about your position."

Still, it takes two to tango, another focus group participant reminded the group. "You have to work at that relationship," he suggested, noting that it depends on the willingness of both parties to be honest with one another and, "give to meet someone else's needs. I think you hit on all eight cylinders together for awhile, and then a year later, or even six months later, you could be hitting on only three cylinders together."

Several career APs recalled portions of their careers when they worked with a disjointed team, or were at loggerheads with their principal or associate APs. One career AP recalled his unhappiness working with a principal who was nearing retirement and unwilling to take a stand. He said he felt like he had "no control over [his] own time," and was "totally at everyone else's mercy."

Another woman said faculty surveys pointed to some deep-rooted problems at her school. "It's been pretty rocky at times," she said, explaining that the faculty did not see the administrative team as a cohesive group. "Part of it is that he [the principal] doesn't delegate well. And that's all right," she said in one breath, but explained in the next how she reacted when faculty came to her with questions for which she had no answers. "I can't tell them if I don't know," she said. "And if I don't know I'm not going to tell them differently. I just say, 'Go tell Hank that you asked me.'"

Career APs who have a good measure of autonomy most often enjoy good relationships with their principals, as well. In addition, these individuals also seem to be well-satisfied with their positions. Autonomy and job satisfaction seem to go hand-in-hand.

"I have a lot of freedom here," one career AP explained. "I have full control over certain teachers and students here. That's a big reason why I stay where I am. I'm sort of a principal under a principal. So I have the power, the leadership, the responsibilities of lots of principals. I even make more money than lots of principals."

Principals are not blind to the importance of their role in shaping the career AP position. Said one, in response to a question about motivation: "I think it is an internal thing . . . that he sees it as an important job. I hope in part because I make him feel that he is important. And then I've encouraged him to take initiative to do things, to check it out and let me know what he's doing, but at the same time I've given him a certain degree of freedom. . . ."

Another said his leadership style was to delegate responsibilities and then hold his APs (three of them, two of whom were career APs) responsible. "I seldom will interfere," he said, explaining that over the years his career APs "either have been able to adjust their styles of administration to match my expectations, or I have changed my expectations to meet the style of the people in those positions."

Clearly, the precise tasks and roles are less important than the chance to work efficiently and comfortably with a good team and to have some areas of discretion, control, and flexibility.

The foregoing quotes and illustrations provide insights into the nuances of career APs' meaning-making as they shape their tasks. Career APs' tasks and roles usually are explicitly stated. However, their interactions at work are full of daily interpretations.

Through this re-interpreting, career APs revise, renegotiate, and tailor their work. Unlike the stereotype of their role, they say "it's always a new challenge" or "it's never boring."

Perhaps they make it that way and, in the process, find rewards and quiet satisfactions. Perhaps while doing so, career APs craft and tailor workable solutions to the constant stream of problems they confront in the minutiae of every day and in the chronic challenges over the long term in schools.

## Career Assistants' Satisfactions and Rewards

### Rewards in the Work

"I just like being here with kids. I'm in a kids' world. I guess it keeps me going. I just like to be in their world."

▶ *Shaping students' lives.*

When career APs talk about the rewards in their work, the most clear and consistent reply is the satisfaction they get from helping youngsters develop. The greatest pleasure comes from helping the "worst" kids.

As one career AP said, "I get the greatest kick out of seeing problem kids shape up—seeing them graduate, get good reports, grow up. . . ."

Another added, "When those kids come back and see us years later, and it's usually the worst ones in the school, it's because we were probably at times the most stable person in their life. . . . I just knew they didn't have the kind of support at home that my children had. The satisfaction of having a young person come up to you years later and shake your hand and seek you out—sometimes it's the worst kid, that never completed school—but they manage to come back to see you. That is satisfying to me."

Describing the emotions of graduation day, another said, "I get all the hugs!"

▶ *Solving problems.*

The second most dominant pattern in career APs' discussions of the satisfactions on the job is their delight in knowing that they anticipate and prevent problems. They love knowing that they have the ability/connections/skills needed to find solutions.

Ed Stovall said, "I know exactly who to call in central office—I used to work there and know the routines; if there's help to be had, I can get it."

Another discussed the satisfaction of having and using power to get things done. She said, "I love the power—ability to pick up the phone and solve a problem."

A fellow AP said for him it was all about solving problems and making 90 percent of the people happy. Most of all, career APs like being at the center of activity where they can sense problems in the making and get at the work of solving them.

▶ *Helping teachers.*

Defying the stereotype of assistant principals, career APs see themselves as people who do a great deal to help their teacher colleagues. True, many assistants assert that teachers should handle more of the discipline problems in the classroom, saying, for example, "I come down hard on those teachers who have an inordinate number of referrals."

Many career APs enjoy helping teachers. Some, like Chester Randall, love the role of being guest lecturer in classrooms. Others, like Edward Stovall, see themselves as instructional consultants, ready to provide empathy, support, and supervision for teachers who seek their help.

Stovall's most treasured resource, he said, was the permanent substitute teachers—reliable, competent, and readily available to be assigned by him wherever they were most needed to keep the instructional program going.

Another career AP recalled the tremendous sense of accomplishment "knowing I helped someone through being a first-year teacher. I work intensively with teachers, encouraging and shaping teachers who received bad evaluations—the satisfaction in seeing improvement."

Career APs can invest time in teachers' development, knowing that good teachers, ultimately, make their work easier. Several career APs said the work was rewarding because it allowed them to be "a member of a team," including teachers, administrators, and the whole array of support staff.

Another rewarding aspect of their work, not on the list of duties, is helping teachers through personal crises. Career APs often get satisfaction when they can help a colleague through coping with a death in the family, major illnesses, divorce, or other crises. Schools sometimes become second families for the adults who work there; personal lives intertwine with work performance but, in addition, career APs devise methods for conveying concern and caring for teachers.

Ed Stovall phones teachers who have called in sick, asking about their health. He explained, "They may think I'm intruding or investigating, but I truly want to know if they're okay. Besides, I need to know so I can assess how long to plan for substitutes."

Where the planning and controlling ends and the sympathy and concern begins is hard to discern.

▶ *Control of the culture.*

One award-winning career AP said he loved "knowing you set the tone for the day."

Fred Meece's system of morning announcements was tone-setting. He managed the announcements, but students and teachers did the talking, sending messages about the Friday dance, but also deeper messages about student and teacher leadership.

Another career AP talked about the satisfaction he got from having "the freedom to move about the building and see good things going on and giving pats on the back." Such back-patting was one in his array of methods to monitor and guide school activities in the "right direction."

One award-winning career AP gained satisfaction from the knowledge that he was a force for stability and for making things work. Another award winner said his satisfactions come from seeing things go well and knowing that your practice and planning made that happen. These career APs have a strong inner sense that they make a difference.

Probably the best summary statement about rewards and satisfactions came from an award winner who said, "Some of our biggest gripes are the very same things that cause us to like to do the job . . . the fact that we have our hands in a lot of different things; we can't possibly get bored." Career APs like being "on the edge," and most speak of theirs as a constantly changing and challenging job.

*Preserving Time for a Personal Life*

Even though the job is a demanding one, many career APs believe their career choice is the most logical because it allows them to retain some control over their personal lives. In many instances, upward mobility would mean having to move the family and dedicate still more time to the job.

Increasing pressure to earn a doctorate places an additional burden on educators who aspire to higher positions. Finding time for coursework and studying is not easy for any full-time administrator, but it is particularly difficult for two-career families where the tasks of parenting and household management must be shared. Single parents find "spare" time even harder to come by. As a result, the aspiring, single parent administrator may shy away from higher positions altogether.

For these and other reasons, several career APs said that their decision to stay in their current positions was based on their desire to maintain the stability and integrity of their family life.

One career AP explained: "Both of my kids went to school here and I got to see them star in athletics, in academics. . . . I had other opportunities but didn't want to move."

This man went on to describe how much his community means to him. In addition, he said, an excellent salary, support for his professional association work, recognition awards and ceremonies, and congenial working conditions keep him quite satisfied.

A colleague said that one of his great satisfactions also was personal. "My oldest daughter likes my being there, and I think our father-daughter relationship has become a lot stronger. . . ."

Two women career APs concurred. One explained that having her children in her own school meant she knew who they were with and what was going on. "They're at activities with me, and I can support them."

The other said, "It gives you the best of both worlds. You have a career and yet you're the Beaver Cleaver mother because you know everything."

A survey respondent said her work life was eased by having her son in the same school because it helps "that he understands how my work can be frantic sometimes and that there are times when my home life is limited."

Grandchildren also can make the career AP position attractive. Marie Miller withdrew her name as a candidate for principal at a neighboring school because, she said, "I thought—do I want that responsibility of the final decision if I am thinking that I want more time with my grandchildren. The two don't exactly go together. . . . Travel [something else she is able to enjoy as a career AP] can wait, but the grandchildren won't wait."

Neither will young children. One man said he wouldn't consider a move up to principal until his children were grown, because he thought, "You literally have to be married to your building if you're going to do a good job as a principal."

Even an unmarried career AP may choose to remain in the position because it affords a sense of family. Going to school activities and seeing "the good kids" develop socially at dances, win wrestling matches, and take home "firsts" in school debates can create a sense of belonging and connection that are not easily replaced. Several noted that "becoming like family" can also be a burden (i.e., when going to the grocery store or even the mailbox requires putting on one's AP persona).

Having a career as a parent can also be tough on youngsters. With both pride and affection in his voice, one man described his son's reaction to his parents' forbidding him to go out with friends on a school night. After stomping upstairs to report the "no go" to a friend waiting on the telephone, the frustrated young man came back down to offer this observation: "It's a hell of a thing being the son of an assistant principal and a teacher. You can't get away with anything."

Another career AP said he didn't think it was fair to his children or to himself because he was always worried that some disgruntled student might take his aggression out on his children. In addition, he worried that his children would be treated differently by teachers because their father was the AP.

Many career APs observed that the tug between school and home is particularly difficult for women administrators. Many leave the high school level because they feel a real crunch at home, one focus group discussant said.

"They'd come in crying over choices they had to make between their job and their children," he continued. "And they were feeling guilty that they weren't good mothers and they weren't good administrators, and they were better than anybody on both counts."

His school district had worked hard to recruit women to be assistant principals and principals at the high school level, "but every one of those efforts has failed because they've opted first for middle school, elementary school, and the central office where they got their life back. Until society can deal with that issue, I think we're going to have a real problem."

Of course, there are women who prefer high school students—women like Mary Alice Kincaid, who turned a deaf ear on overtures for her to apply for other positions over the years. "I really like high school people better," she said, recalling that the assistant superintendent couldn't believe it when she told him she wasn't interested in an elementary school principalship.

Another woman advised her colleagues that they only had to look at who attended state association meetings to get a sense of the gender troubles facing education. "I go, and I'm the token female," she told those seated around the table. "My kids are old enough so that I can go off, and it's not a big deal. But when you have 9, 10, and 11-year-olds, you don't go off and leave them with Dad at work. The participation of women outside their own school is severely restricted, too, because of that same reason. We just can't pull it off because we're still the primary caregivers. That's the bottom line."

Clearly, both men and women experience role conflict, but the demands and the norms of the administrative career create more role conflicts for women. Helgesen (1990) found that, where women can integrate the domestic sphere with their career roles, they are more able to have a satisfactory career.

Most career APs do find ways to combine their personal lives with their professional duties. Many have spouses who are teachers; they talk about the comfort they derive from coming home to someone who understands the complexity and stress of their job. They take their children and spouses with them as they supervise games, concerts, plays, and dances in the evenings.

Staying in the AP position does not eliminate role conflicts. One career AP missed all his son's football games while he supervised his own school's games. Another noted that, in his district, the amount of time spent on the job was leading to an increase in divorces, family counseling, and "kids feeling that they're being left out while you deal with 1,200 other kids."

Still, career APs generally agreed that their positions had real advantages when they wanted to stay closely connected with their children's development; avoid having to move the family; reserve time for leisure, friends, and hobbies; and "be there" for family. For those with grown children and for the unmarried career AP, the position was valued as one that allowed for a more normal and balanced life. Most career APs had carefully compared their job to central office staff, principal, and superintendent positions, and they could detail the myriad reasons why theirs was preferable.

*Developing Methods for Stress Management*

Most career APs have a well-developed set of outside activities that provide relaxation and needed diversion from their jobs. They said, for example, "I do aerobics," or, "For me, it's woodworking." Others mentioned hiking, golf, etc. Even those who do not have such outlets are very aware of the pressing need for such diversions. They openly discuss the physical and emotional repercussions—e.g., high blood pressure, weight gain, headaches, and stomach problems—that befall those who can't get away from the job.

*The Values, Philosophies, and Priorities of the Career AP*

"I don't believe in selling my soul to the school. I believe in enjoying what I'm doing, and in doing the very best job I can do for kids. It gives you pleasure to see them in progress. There are lots of failures, too, but you still keep trying. You don't give up on them."

The shaping of the career assistant principal begins at birth. Values and life philosophies, although shaped by training and professional experience, have their roots in childhood. For the most part, these professionals attest to having a clear-cut set of standards. Often, they have had to work hard to achieve the financial security and professional respect.

One New England administrator attributes his high standards and get-it-done-now workstyle to the way he was brought up. Speaking about his father, he said, "There were expectations. You met those expectations, and that was that. I started working at age 12. My family was struggling when I was small."

Randall's early self-sufficiency has served him well as a career AP. "He is motivated intrinsically and will take initiative," according to his principal.

Noting that every AP is unique, he said Randall looks at the assistant principalship as a profession. "He likes kids, and has his own zany sense of humor. They respond to it. He's positive."

The spouse of another career AP attributes his wife's success with students to four factors: intelligence, integrity, empathy, and rapport with a wide range of people. He believes his wife's rapport with students and parents alike stems from the fact that she is "basically so fair," a trait she learned as a child.

*Caring Through Discipline*

"My job is really tough. These aren't my problems, but I'm caught in the middle. I'm the mediator. Take the kid who goes to one class and he's an angel. Then, three classes later, he's a devil. What happened? This business of discipline is complex."

Nowhere are the values of empathy, rapport, and fairness more evident or necessary than in the realm of discipline—a category of activity that requires the wisdom of Solomon, the adeptness of Mercury, and the cleverness of Ulysses, depending on the circumstances at hand.

Discipline can range from convincing an out-of-control young lady to stop throwing chairs in the cafeteria to breaking up a knife fight. It can mean dealing with a youngster who tells her bus mate, "I'm going to beat you up," or calling parents to inform them marijuana has been found in their son's locker.

Philosophies about discipline are as varied as the career APs charged with exercising it. For some, discipline is most effective when it's immediate.

For others, it's a question of discretion and flexibility. "You use your ability to call the situation. . . . The student is out of control, the teacher is upset. . . . You know it's about being calmed down and understanding what are correct and acceptable procedures so that the student can go on with his education. That's what it's all about."

One thing that all the career APs we talked with agree on is that young people have changed during the last two decades.

Michael Sullivan believes that much of the difference can be attributed to television. "TV's probably our worst enemy," he says, explaining that students come to the classroom expecting to be entertained. The challenge for schools, then, is to motivate students accustomed to a TV culture.

Sullivan runs into problems, he says, when teachers confuse educational issues with disciplinary problems. "I consider everything that I do instructional," he continues. "But some people try to separate discipline from instruction, and that's where we have a big problem."

Daily, Sullivan sees students who have been reported for failing to dress for gym, for not responding to a math question, for refusing to read aloud in class. "I don't think we can do anything to make kids learn. They have to want to learn. Being able to inspire people is what separates the average teacher from the exceptional teacher."

Important at all age levels, being fair to students can sometimes pose ethical dilemmas. A career AP can get caught between doing what he or she believes is in a student's best interest, or supporting a teacher's interpretation of school policy. The scenario usually entails a teacher reporting a student for an infringement of either classroom or official school policy. According to the letter of the law, the teacher is perfectly justified in issuing the disciplinary notice. It falls to the career AP to administer the appropriate punishment.

Mary Alice Kincaid remembers one such incident as if it were yesterday, even though it occurred 11 years ago, during her first year as an assistant principal. The situation involved two ninth-grade girls—both of them good students—and a first-year teacher. It was school policy that students shouldn't talk during exams, and if they did, their tests would be taken and their grades lowered by 20 percent.

After turning in their papers, these two young ladies made the mistake of taking out a cookie and sharing both it and some whispered conversation. Whammo, the teacher wrote them up and sent the disciplinary notice to Ms. Kincaid. The minute she received it, she was troubled, because she felt the penalty did not fit the infringement, and that lowering the girls' grades would not reflect what they had learned during the semester.

"I don't think that discipline, as far as we can control it, should affect grades," she said, recalling the incident and pointing out that they were only ninth graders and it was their first exam, a two-hour exam, at that. "It was not cheating, it was discipline," a point Ms. Kincaid suggested to the teacher, but he was not about to change his mind.

Ms. Kincaid worked for several weeks to find a solution. She was torn between her desire to back the teacher, particularly since it was his first year of teaching, and her conviction that the girls were being wronged. Lurking below the surface was the fact that the teacher was a black man in a predominantly white school. "I think he felt that some of the white people weren't working with him, and I didn't want that to go on."

In the end, a compromise was reached. The girls wrote a paper, but were allowed to keep the grades they would have earned had the incident not occurred. Ms. Kincaid says she doesn't really know what finally brought the teacher around.

"Persistence, maybe," she speculates.

Reflecting on the incident, she says, "You don't know what the right thing is all the time, but you do the very best that you can with each situation."

Sometimes such incidents contain all the ingredients of a principal's nightmare. "I can see the headlines now," chuckled Michael Sullivan, relating an incident he succeeded in resolving between interviews the day we visited his school.

It seems a teacher, an about-to-graduate senior and his family, and the school had locked horns over the teacher's insisting the student serve a 15-minute detention for leaving class to go to the bathroom. According to Sullivan, the teacher had a behavior management plan that required students to "pay back the time" if they left class to go to the bathroom.

In effect all year, Sullivan concedes that the policy "may have been a good one, but somehow it wasn't communicated to the parent." As a result, the student's furious mother was first referred to Sullivan's co-assistant principal, who made no headway. Next, the principal met with her. The principal referred the case to Sullivan. He assessed the situation and determined that it was essentially a power struggle between the teacher, the student, and the parent. Armed with that knowledge, Sullivan said he knew what he had to do, and that was to let everyone save face.

His solution? "To make it a timeout-type issue and not a discipline-type issue."

Toward the end of the day, we found Sullivan sitting in his office with the student, having a friendly conversation about what he was going to do after graduation, what his brothers were up to, and so on. They had already agreed that the student would report to study hall 15 minutes early the next day.

Summing up what had happened after the boy left, Sullivan explained that, "Sometimes you can't solve a problem, but you can compromise with all the individuals involved and come out with a solution that satisfies everybody. Although you didn't solve the problem, it looks like you did. In reality, I didn't do much of anything but have some dialog with the student."

Such vignettes give life to the task called "discipline" that takes up so much of any AP's time. They demonstrate the values embedded in the thinking and actions of discipline; these educators' disciplinary actions are carried out in ways that exhibit a deep caring about young people's development. Career APs not only find kids' progress to be rewarding, they articulate a well-developed understanding of the connection between discipline, development, and caring.

## Working Behind the Scenes

"You use your ability to call the situation: the student is out of control, the teacher is upset. You know it's about being calmed down and understanding what are correct and acceptable procedures so the student can go on with his education. That's what it's all about."

"Calling the situation" is second nature for career APs. Some of these seasoned administrators have been in the community so long that, when faced with a situation requiring quick judgment, they can call upon their knowledge of a student's family resources. Or, they may have private information about the kinds of stress a certain teacher is facing. A behind-the-scenes work mode seldom provides tangible rewards, honors, or promotions. Nevertheless, career APs seem to prefer this mode. The payoff is the chance to exercise discretion and to make judgment calls as they create their unique ways of performing their tasks.

▶  *Discretion and flexibility.*

"She just handles everything. She doesn't ever need to ask for help. She just does it, and sometimes she does things and we didn't even know she did them. Everybody just knows that she'll handle it the best. . . ."

"The best thing the principal does for an assistant is to define the job and then let him do it without petty interference," said a seasoned educator, a 56-year-old who, as teacher and AP, had worked with 10 principals.

Many principals recognize that truth. Said one suburban principal who had three assistants, "It was either make them turn in a direction that they weren't comfortable going just to meet my ego, my own self-perception of an administrator, or adjust that perception enough to allow them their space to do their thing and still get the job done."

The most satisfied career APs are those who enjoy freedom from supervision. As long-time, trusted, and loyal members of a team, they exercise discretion in literally hundreds of situations every day.

Edward Stovall compared his current career AP position with his years as a central office supervisor, and said that he now has much more power and freedom where it counts—in affecting the instruction and the students. In central office, he said, "You have to work collegially and negotiate everything."

➤ *Aversion to controversy.*

"That's a good point, that safety valve thing, because we have a lot of responsibility and make decisions every day. But the final decision is made by the principal."

Having worked with a number of principals, career APs have observed how that position works for people. Many career APs have well-articulated comparisons to demonstrate that the assistant principalship is the more desirable position. A few even know what it feels like to sit in the principal's chair as acting principal for several months.

"I know how hard I work as an assistant principal," shared one career AP. "But the intensity of the principal's job is even more so, because more difficult decisions at a higher level come to that desk every day. There are more decisions and more political pressures."

Agreeing, another added, "we have a nice cushion, protected from the board, the superintendent." The three APs in Tom Meece's school, in their daily luncheon meeting, said, "Principals cannot make mistakes but we can, and we do make lots of mistakes!"

Career APs learn over time to avoid risky, threatening, or controversial behavior, and to develop in themselves a sense that they can do more for kids by working behind the scenes.

➤ *Feeling powerful but free of politics.*

"I do scheduling, counseling. We decide who teaches what, when they teach it, where they teach it. We get the best teachers, and the kids' requests, and the principals' demands, and I meld those together. We don't have to worry about the school board members. I never see them. Yet, I know we set the tone of the school."

In the focus group interviewing, one assistant said, "We have power and we love it. This is a powerful position."

The statement provoked controversy and debate, but she persisted, explaining, "It's raw power. I think it's flattering when people come to your office with a problem, and you can pick up the phone and call the police department, or social services, and say, 'This is the assistant principal and I need a little help, and I'd kind of like you to come by.'"

During the debate that followed, several career APs picked up on her thinking: "There are two kinds of power. The principal has power because of his position. We have power because of what we do. Now, the position itself is powerless; the principal can overrule us any day. But, because of our effectiveness in the position, we've pulled a whole lot of that power into ourselves. It just happens. It's not because we're saying 'this will get us power.'"

This power and freedom must not become too visible or wayward, and unpopular values must be carefully managed. Edward Stovall provided this insight when he said, "You have to be a team player and learn how to voice your opinion with the game plan."

Career APs enjoy being able to talk and act in ways that are, in their eyes, more free than the principal. It is important to note, though, that the early career intentions of many career APs included moving to a principalship.

➤ *Being outspoken.*

Speaking about his willingness to intervene quickly, Barney Harris said that even when he did not have all the facts, "I'd rather be a bull in a china shop than sit back and wonder if I'm doing the right thing, because I'll be more likely to help the kid or fix the situation fast."

In several instances, career APs' colleagues and principals made strong suggestions that the AP was in the right niche because he or she was too blunt, or would tend to take on everything and offend some people.

Edward Stovall, reflecting on the portrayal of career APs, said, "Make sure you recognize that some do not move up because they have problems communicating with their colleagues."

Comments such as these suggest that some career APs speak out, bluntly, in ways they feel are important for kids or for the school, but that would be viewed as undesirable in a principal.

Bullheaded yet avoiding controversy; caring about young people by disciplining them; searching for "fair" solutions to dilemmas, yet often making snap judgments. Career APs are complex and sometimes contradictory individuals.

At 8 a.m., a career AP may punish a whole class for one kid's stink bomb, showing no mercy. Two hours later, at 10:30 a.m., that same person has turned into a patient, skillful committee chair who guides 10 professionals through 20 minutes of deliberation to develop a plan for one at-risk child!

Individual career APs are as different in style and personality as the handwoven scarves and tapestries of skilled weavers. But just as one or two threads can anchor a weaving and give it unity and strength, so, too, a consistent pattern emerges with career assistant principals. That pattern emerges from the skillful weaving of personal life values and career satisfactions to create an educator who is a major contributor to the development of young people and the stability and success of his or her school.

# Chapter III
# How Programs and Policies Affect the Career Assistant Principal

Those who search for ways to support good school management need insights about how programs and policies affect the career AP. This section uses the reflections of career APs to identify the kinds of structures, incentives, support, and rewards that are available.

## Site-Based Policies

The most critical policies are those that are played out at the school site. A good relationship with one's principal and a smoothly functioning administrative team can make all the difference in the world, not just to the individuals involved, but to the school as a whole.

One school in the study exuded an almost tangible air of warmth and welcome from the moment the researcher stepped through the front door, a feeling that was reinforced throughout the entire day. The career AP at this school gave all the credit to her principal, a woman who "just creates a friendly, accepting, warm atmosphere."

In contrast, a focus group participant who prides herself on being "pretty good at getting to know people," zeroed in on how a career AP's role can change when the principal fails to encourage a good working partnership.

"I was fortunate enough to be working on a team last year, but this year I'm not," she recounted. "This principal does not believe that we're a team. . . . It the principal isn't going to at least allow some conversations, it isn't going to happen. It doesn't matter how open you want to be, if the principal isn't open, you're not going to get anyplace."

Supportive principals know this intuitively. Said one who "inherited" a career AP when she was transferred to a new school: "We did a lot of talking the summer before I began to try and make sure we were on the same wave length, because there were so many things that I did differently from my predecessors. You have to have a common philosophy. Your philosophy's the most important thing, because it undergirds everything that you do."

Another focus group participant observed that whereas schools used to be run like a "mom and pop" business, today they are sophisticated organizations. The old "this is my castle; I am the principal" style of leadership no longer works, he asserted.

"I think administrators realize that they have to build a leadership team . . . that they can't promote effective change or effective programs in their buildings solely by themselves."

The role of the AP, he continued, is to serve as "sort of a Polaroid filter that makes things a little bit clearer. You can bring things into a little finer focus because there are two of you or three of you working together as a leadership team."

Positive reinforcement from a principal can have an impact on both performance and morale. The principal of one career AP who loves her job responded this way to a question about motivation: "I think we get a lot of strokes here, from one another and from the staff. We get it from the students, too; and we get it from one another. There is certainly a mutual admiration society here."

On the other hand, the principal of a school where the career AP feels somewhat isolated openly stated that he would never deliberately look for somebody who wanted to be a career assistant principal. "I don't think," he elaborated, "that they are going to provide as much leadership, as much creativity or innovation, as much of themselves as someone who is actively seeking to learn all they can learn about administration, in preparation for their own school."

Does that attitude get communicated to the career AP? Chances are, it does; as much by what is said as by what is left unsaid.

In another principal's words, "It doesn't matter if the whole world is complimenting you; if a person doesn't feel like it's enough, then it's not enough. The person's own perception is the most important thing."

*Flexibility, Pet Projects, and Discretion*

Career APs often can develop special projects and distinctive skills or expertise. Flexibility and discretion in their daily work allows them to develop skills as a computer expert, to be creative with a special project, or to set up a scheme to channel problem students' energies. The longevity, accumulated trust, and long-term commitment to their schools and the ability to shape some of their work routines pays off for career APs. They earn the flexibility and discretion to invent and create.

Randall's pet projects were students, or rather, individualized programs for selected students. He explained how he identified 10 to 15 "unpopular, funny-looking, out-of-it kids" and groomed them for student government. "I always make sure that some of my kids get elected," he said.

For one middle school boy with "a horrible home life, who is so full of anger that he sometimes lets loose," Randall created a punching bag out of insulation stored in the school's storage area.

Barney Harris's pet project, an adult education program, was so much a part of his agenda that he was planning to work at it full-time upon retirement. He left no stone unturned; at graduation, he told a personal story about each individual, garnered from countless hours of sleuthing and phone conversations. The program was *his* initiative, created to represent his values about service to the community. It was under his control, and was highly visible to the entire community.

That he seldom asked Board approval, that this was a communitywide program, that he was sole director with a loyal, seasoned, and satisfied staff—all these factors added to his satisfaction.

Special projects and areas of discretion and distinction provide career APs with opportunities to be creative.

## At the District Level and Beyond

District, professional, association, and other related forces can make the career AP's job easier. Clear patterns were these:

➤ *Consistent policy from above.*

Not only do career APs like predictable environments, much of the satisfaction they get from their jobs is based on their ability to keep the school environment stable and predictable. Ambiguity and vacillation in program policies cause tremendous distress for all educators. Career APs feel special frustration, since their effectiveness revolves around the trust built up over time in their relationships at work.

➤ *Non-interference with their job.*

When asked about how district policies and their principal help them in their work, career APs frequently replied, "By leaving me alone to do my job!"

➤ *Supporting professional affiliations.*

The highest paid and perhaps most satisfied career AP in this study, Fred Meece, described his involvement in an array of professional activities at the district, state, and national levels. His district has a policy providing for paid sabbaticals for administrators (mostly for pursuing doctoral studies); it pays expenses for trips to professional conferences; and allows ample time away from school activities when he serves in official capacities in professional associations. Such policies, even when career APs do not take full advantage (some feel they just cannot be away from their school) are appreciated. However, they are not available in many districts.

District support and time away from schools for conferences can provide meaningful support to the career APs' sense of professionalism.

Assistant principals belong to NASSP more frequently than other associations, but they also list the Association for Curriculum Development and their state and local administrators' associations among an array of others. Some belong primarily because they want the publications.

➤ *Salary, benefits, rewards, and awards.*

Salary increases do matter. All the intrinsic rewards derived by inventive and self-sustaining career APs cannot make them forget salary schedules.

In this study, salaries ranged from about $40,000 to nearly $80,000 per year. But in the eyes of career APs, their comparison groups are the principals and teachers in their own districts, not those of other assistant principals in far-away states or very different districts.

The suburban career APs are less concerned about the higher salary of the AP in a high school with 1,200 inner-city students than they are about whether they make more than their own teacher colleagues. Many assert that, because of their year-round contracts and their after-school supervision duties, they earn less than teachers. Some complain that the gap between principal and assistant principal salaries is too wide. The perception of several career APs was that principals typically make $1,000 to $4,000 more than APs.

Good salaries keep career APs feeling happy where they are. A few districts recognize and pay for the special contributions of the career AP by paying a special supplement to the AP of five or more years. The bottom line is, the bottom line does count.

➤ *Symbols and ceremonies count, too.*

It makes a difference when a school board hosts an elegant dinner for the educators and spouses who have stayed in the district for a number of years, or for when APs are selected by their state associations as APs of the year. The impact of these awards can be heightened when state legislatures and local districts send congratulations.

### Recruitment and Selection Policies

District policies for recruitment and selection are carried out in the context of state policies that set certification requirements, including a minimum number of years of teaching, a master's degree, and certification. Usually, the certification requirements for APs and principals are the same.

Details of recruitment and selection policies in several districts point to certain trends. One southern principal said, "It used to be that the superintendent would sit back in his chair and roll images of people before him and say, yeah, I think he would be good for the job." Several career APs described how the "Good Old Boy" system used to work, helping those with social contacts get access and training and a network for attaining positions.

Most agree that a more technical approach is followed in districts now, but there were conflicting views about whether the more formal training, recruitment, and selection processes were improvements.

One career AP openly asserted, "I'd have fared very well if we'd kept the good old boy system." A number of administrators in his district had moved up via participation in an innovative staff development program. The district began using the NASSP Assessment Center as part of recruitment. Interviews involving central office and site personnel would result in recommendations of the top three candidates, from which the Board would make selections.

A similar process in Fred Meece's district was creating new tensions, as he and his then smooth-working and happy team anticipated the arrival of a new AP following the transfer of one of their current APs to a central office position.

Putting selection of APs in the hands of central office staff and using more technical tools to assess candidates are considered to be methods for increasing professionalism and equity. However, it removes some important discretion and control from the site.

*Assessment and Evaluation*

Principals evaluate APs, sometimes with the assistant of procedures like assessment centers. Some career APs talked about assessment centers as the best thing the district offered for training, but others had negative reactions.

Michael Sullivan's principal, who raved about Michael's special contributions and qualities ("The less tangible factors like loyalty to the community and rapport with local leaders and community members") said they would never be noticed in a formal assessment tool. "When you go out and compete in the broader arena, those specialized strengths sometimes get lost," he said.

Randall's assessment center results indicated that he needed to work on using more cautious, deliberative decision making. He had received the same advice from his first principal; now, a few years from retirement, he was still getting the same advice.

Sullivan's principal presented a nice summary of how the new assessment and evaluation efforts have affected career APs, saying: "A certain group came into administration when experience and loyalty were the most important factors, and then they ran into the new theme of objective standards of ability. It's like 'you're playing by new rules now.' This caught a number of folks mid-game."

### Training, Internships, Staff Development

Training targeted to assistant principal tasks, while rare, is the most meaningful for career APs. None reported having internships focusing on the AP position. Those who had internships were grouped together with those aiming toward principalships and central office positions, so they were exposed to districtwide experiences. The districtwide perspective helped them to know they preferred the AP position, and gave them a range of people to call upon when they needed a resource for their school.

When asked about training and staff development for assistants, Barney Harris pondered, searched his memory, and finally said, "How about the state-sponsored training for student assistant team; would that fit?"

Chester Randall's district had two to three-year internships for aspiring administrators, but it was geared to those who would be principals and superintendents.

Career APs benefit from and enjoy conferences and workshops designed especially for them. A recent phenomenon, these conferences are usually sponsored by state administrators' associations. There was no mention of instances of district, university, or state department of education-sponsored staff development or training for assistant principals.

### What Helps Most

When asked, "What helps you most in getting through your day and over the long haul?" there were certain answers that stood out. They included: "My Christian belief that in 'doing unto others . . .' helps me take the anger out of my behavior"; "My own upbringing"; and "longevity." One found his military and seminary training most helpful.

More typical answers were "My sense of humor"; "The trust level with staff and students"; "My positive outlook on things, and my wife, friends, and family"; "Positive interaction with students and teachers"; "The challenge and variety"; "My organizational skills"; and last but certainly not least, "My principal."

*Professional Associations*

When career APs were asked to talk about professional association, university, and state department of education contributions to their well-being, they focused on professional associations. NASSP received most commendations for their supportive programs and policies, including high praise for their awards and special publications, and especially for focusing on assistants.

One said, "They've valued the assistant principalship as a career position." (Keep in mind that the entire sample of 50 career APs in this study were NASSP members.)

Universities were only mentioned in connection with particularly helpful individuals; no university programs were lauded. Coursework was generally seen as irrelevant. Only one person said the universities and state department of education, along with professional associations, were helpful. This individual mentioned helpful courses, seminars, workshops, professional advice and legal counsel, and clarification of laws affecting tasks like special education implementation and discipline.

Their state and local professional associations get credit for helping assistants in the following ways; educating the board and the superintendent on the importance of the AP; recognizing that the assistant is a valid career position, not just an assistant to the principal; involving assistants in activity at the state level; and negotiating salary and benefits, and representing them in matters of concern about their job.

*Helpful and Supportive Programs and Policies*

"Give me a task, give me direction, and give me room to work," was a characteristic career AP reply to the survey's query about how the district, superintendent, or principal helped APs. One respondent said she was not aware of any ways the district or superintendent helped assistants!

The individual within the district who receives the most credit for being helpful is the principal. Typical phrases were: "By being a good role model and providing career counseling"; "Shows appreciation for my dedication"; and "My principal encourages my professional development."

Principals received the most credit for helping, not by creating supportive policies or programs, but by teaming, advising, supporting, and allowing flexibility. Of course, principals can set that tone when district policies support principals for being that way.

In fact, superintendents received little mention or credit. One respondent who did mention the superintendents' responsibility for helpful actions, programs, and policies said: "He guided me to authors, speakers, and concepts that provided inspiration."

However, districts (presumably under the superintendent's direction) received honorable mention for helpful programs and policies in the following descriptions: "They hired clerical help for paperwork; off-duty police for security; and instituted site-based management teams." "We get $500 a year that we can spend any way we want: materials, convention, books." "Giving APs with more than five years $1,500 more per year."

Career APs value district support for attending professional meetings and state conferences designed especially for assistants. One career AP said, with excitement, "I'm going to a state conference next week, and they are paying my way, too. I seldom have to come up with any kind of money. That's a tremendous lift!"

Said another, "Now assistants are part of the district leadership team, and they've moved the meetings so we can attend. So now we're included in some planning, whereas before we were just implementers."

Although this practice is more prevalent in larger schools with more than one AP, some districts still include the assistants from single-AP schools on administrative councils.

*Essential Policies*

Some work patterns, programs, and policies are essential. Without them, the job would be intolerable.

➤ *Breaks from routines.*

In a discussion among career APs, one veteran advised, "People, you'd better take your vacation days. Close your doors for half an hour a day. Otherwise they'll burn you out." The advice was offered to the focus group as they talked about how hard it was to get away, and how they had to increase their workloads when state or district funding constraints left needs unmet and work undone.

They described dire circumstances: 4 administrators doing the work of 10; managing year-round schools on 10-month contracts; and cutting personnel, clerical workers, and custodians.

This list illustrates how policy changes—e.g., budget cuts, year-round schools, cutting the administrative staff—could make the career AP position intolerable. The intensity and stress of the job cannot be borne without breaks.

▶ *Flexibility, communication, and autonomy.*
Career APs, in interviews and on surveys, repeatedly assert that their job is made possible and satisfying by the fact that they are left alone to do their job. They also stress, strongly, the value of good communication with other site administrators. Any policies and procedures that support good communication and allow flexibility and autonomy, then, are essential to the work of the career AP.

## Policies That Disrupt

Restructuring and site-based management policies have thrown the career APs' role into turmoil. Snippets from a conversation among APs revealed their sentiments: "We dabble with site-based management; I get so frustrated. The principal puts out an issue for the teachers to come up with a solution. . . . Now, I ask you, who's going to implement the solution? Me! And I wasn't involved in the process. That drives me nuts."

Another responded, "We're left out of the loop."

Still another said, "It's just assumed that teachers will come up with the idea and I'll take care of it when they're done deciding. . . . I have no problem with that if I'm part of the decision to start with."

It became almost a chorus: "They're empowering teachers to order us around."

This conversation flowed naturally to a related discussion about the "psychological undermining" that results from being required to attend and manage inservice and other after-hours work for no extra pay.

"It's lack of professional respect. Teachers, even central office staff, sell tickets at games and get paid for it, but we don't."

Several commented that they had "taken care of that" in negotiations. Others pointed out that in their states it was illegal to be unionized. The reply was, "We're not unionized . . . we just negotiated, and they gave it to us."

Such flowing conversations focus on policy, highlighting both the similarities and the differences in the ways policies affect APs. Clearly, though, current state and district policy thrusts have disruptive effects on their established roles and understanding about how to proceed with their work.

## Unrecognized Sources of Support

▶  *Good secretaries.*

This was the strongly voiced reply to the query asking about the unrecognized people who make the career AP's work easier and more satisfying. Career APs, when asked, said secretaries make their lives more pleasant by "being efficient and loyal," "by believing in me," and "by taking care of tasks that are boring to me."

Other answers listed groups, including aides, other APs, and guidance counselors who, for example, "help calm angry parents, talk to students about conflict, come prepared for work, and are available to discuss school problems."

One said his life was made more satisfying and pleasant by the principal, department heads, maintenance staff, coaches, and secretaries "when they write notes of encouragement, give nice Christmas gifts, and tell me they appreciate me."

Teachers make career APs' work lives more satisfying, easier, and more pleasant by doing their jobs well. One spoke of the satisfaction of working with teachers in training for leadership, saying how pleasant it is since they are "open-minded, willing to learn, and supportive of management."

## Administrative Career Policies and Trends

Certain norms, new trends, and chronic problems in school administration have particular effects on career APs.

## Doctorates, Turnover, and Moving Vans

Increasingly, administrators with doctorates and a willingness to move are the ones regarded as having special potential for higher administrative careers. Educators who are unwilling to uproot personal and family lives may encounter barriers to upward mobility. Some APs become career APs, in part, because the chance for upward mobility is not worth the expense and disruption of holding their job and working toward a doctorate.

As Chester Randall said, "I could have done it, and I was halfway there but it wasn't worth it."

Fred Meece, AP for 16 years, and Richard Adams, AP for 22 years, decided to stay after seeing that moving up would require moving their families. Each had had opportunities.

Adams said, "I've seen others who've moved around, and they've suffered the hazards with their kids." He continued, "Eventually, the doctorate became important; I did all the coursework, but then they closed the doctoral program. I inquired at another university, but that would have cost more money." These setbacks convinced Adams to settle into the career AP position.

Finally, the days of longevity in principalships and superintendencies are waning. In some districts, they're long gone.

Edward Stovall's experience of having two superintendents in the last eight years is increasingly common. He said, "You don't get any mentoring from central office in these circumstances because everyone's worrying about their own jobs."

Still, slower turnover occurs at lower administrative ranks, and APs often become career APs simply because no one is moving.

► *Sexism.*

Not a policy, and certainly not a new issue, sexism rears its head when men resist change and undermine women's leadership opportunities.

Edward Stovall predicted that several administrators would leave rather than work with a woman superintendent. This kind of thinking carries over to affect career APs.

One career AP said, "If you see another AP doing something wrong, you give advice but you don't go to his principal." Others agreed with her that APs stick together and informally train each other, but they do not tell on each other. Thus, chronic issues like sexism are left to fester.

► *Low turnover and the preference for "new blood."*

Although districts vary, opportunities for promotion are rare in some districts. Two trends affect career APs: low growth districts, and districts with policies and practices favoring outsiders ("for new blood.")

Michael Sullivan's principal commented on his district's tendency to prefer outsiders as the population grows and shifts, saying, "There's immigration into this county, both natural and recruited," which devalues the career AP qualities.

Another principal commented, "Longevity and experience in the system are just not as important as they used to be."

► *Salary and role alterations.*

Richard Adams and several others originally entered the AP position partly because it was a sizable salary increase. Now, in many cases, APs see little to no salary incentive to change jobs. In some districts, principals make only $1,000 to $4,000 more than the career AP, not enough difference to entice the true career AP to make the change.

Furthermore, to many a career AP, the principalship is unappealing. Chester Randall said that, with restructuring and intense state involvement in education policy making, "They're turning principals into record-keeping pencil pushers."

His principal predicted problems in recruiting principals, saying, "The principalship looks less desirable now for most people. APs see theirs as a job where they can have some satisfactions and yet not have to accept some of the frustrations that principals might have to accept."

➤ *Expanded roles, rules, and staff.*
"Education has more and more responsibilities now and he has to respond to them," said the educator wife of career AP Barney Harris, referring to the array of social issues connected to schools' missions.

Barney later described how he managed getting a pregnant teen to a gynecologist; getting the girl's unsuspecting mother to the hospital; and serving as family counselor, social worker, and medic through the birth.

He recalled, "That was before there were laws about how to proceed and school teams of professionals to deal with such situations." Years ago, he handled this crisis alone. Now, schools take on more social, family, health, and religious responsibilities. Those teams of professionals, including social workers, psychologists, nurses, special education teachers, guidance counselors, as well as the team of site administrators, share the work through formal weekly meetings and division of responsibilities.

## Preferences for Programs, Policies, and Job Restructuring

"I'd like more time to sit and think and be as creative as I'd like to be. Even in summer we don't have time to retreat and reflect."

Throughout the data-gathering for this study, assistant principals reflected on various ways to improve their positions. Most of their preferences, and their disappointments, can be deduced from the descriptions of policies and programs cited in this monograph. No simple alteration will automatically solve troublesome issues, but a few of their suggestions and poignant appeals are useful.

One said he wanted "more time in the classrooms, seeing the positive side of what goes on in schools."

Ed Stovall said it this way: "I'd like more involvement in instructional supervision; that's where you can make good things happen so there will be fewer discipline problems."

Survey responses included, "I'd like being called 'associate principal . . . that would be a different mindset'"; "Make AP salaries close to equivalent with principals"; "Change the public perception so that it's not viewed as some kind of failure."

Probably the best way to end this report, though, is the quote from an award-winning career AP, as he talked to others in the focus group interview, saying, "I don't think we get the kind of recognition we need, but maybe it's our own damned fault. We have to start beating our own drum—probably through an assistant principal organization."

This study, by exploring and reporting on the daily realities of the lives of career assistant principals, is a good start on the agenda of recognizing their contributions and their needs.

# Appendix A
# Research Methods

The purpose of this study was to provide a portrait and some insights into the lives, the work, and the inner motivations of career assistant principals. Qualitative research such as this gets at insiders' points of view and sets the data-gathering in the natural setting so the interplay of school context, personal interactions, and connections with daily routines are displayed and can be incorporated into the portrait.

This study captured that insiders' view, and also sought expanded clarification and verification using multiple methods to incorporate data from 50 assistant principals. The design, data collection, analysis, and reporting took place from January through July of 1992, carried out by Catherine Marshall with the assistance of Jeanne Steele and with the support of Maryellen Parker, NASSP Director of AP Services, and the NASSP Committee on the Assistant Principalship.

Observation, interviewing, and surveys were used to collect several types of data and to attain information from several different perspectives.

## Step 1: Focus Group Interviews

*(Incorporating 14 people)*

The McDonald's/NASSP National Assistant Principal Recognition Program awards ceremonies provided an opportunity for focus group interviews by convening APs from across the country.

By interviewing groups of individuals with similar or parallel backgrounds, one gets data on shared perspectives and experiences. Participants in the study included AP national winners with 10 or more years of experience, selected members of the NASSP Committee on the Assistant Principalship, and one member of the NASSP Board of Directors. Their experience as APs ranged from 4 to 17 years, and their ages ranged from 43 to 55 years. The two groups included a total of 14 APs, including 10 men and 4 women. One participant was a minority. They came from 13 states and the District of Columbia. Many, but not all the participants were career assistant principals.

These APs knew and trusted each other to the extent that they had shared several days of small conference happenings together. They knew and trusted the researcher to the extent that half had heard her two-hour presentation on the assistant principalship six months earlier. This, and the instruction to speak openly, argue, and differ with each other where appropriate; and to respond to the thematic statements provided as stimuli, allowed open but guided discussion on the assistant principalship. (See Appendix B for the Thematic Statements that were the stimuli for the Focus Group Interviewing.)

Frequently, participants agreed with others' statements and expanded upon them, and important nuances emerged from the two hours' discussions.

For example, the women objected to statements about the advantage of being able to integrate your work and personal life—for them, the integration was either not evident or not easy. They also brought up the problem of getting all the work while male administrators eased off, and not being able to complain about it (complaining about a fellow administrator violates norms of loyalty).

## Step 2: Participant Observation and Interviewing

*(Incorporating 10 people)*

Using mailing lists provided by NASSP, we sent 84 letters to administrators in 10 states, including both coasts, the north, and the south. The letter attached an article describing the typology of assistant principals, and asked the administrators to nominate APs who fit the category of career assistant principal.

Follow-up phone calls and letters were used to verify categorization and schedule appointments. Responses were enthusiastic, although some resisted being put in that category. A final sample of 10 assistants was identified from four states. This group included six men and four women. Four were African Americans. Of the schools visited, four were suburban, two were rural, and two were urban.

Standing next to the AP managing lunch duties, pacing through hall patrol, sitting in on the PST and administrative team meetings, watching the banter with students during bus duty—all provide far better insights than any survey could possibly reveal.

In most cases, we spent an entire work day with an assistant principal, engaging in observation as well as formal and informal interviewing. In all instances, the APs eased the access to their schools and openly displayed their work life.

We recognize that our sample includes the more willing and open APs, so this may be a biased sample, providing insights into the assistant principals who work in the most favorable conditions and those who feel more professional and community support than others.

However, of those who did not want to participate, the reasons given were, for example, "We're moving to a new school"; or, "We're in end-of-year testing"; or, "I don't fit in your category."

As the APs conducted their daily work, they described what they were doing and provided their logic and rationale. Their co-workers often talked about the school, the students, their routines, and the assistant, providing rich contextual data through the course of the day of observation.

Finally, the range of activities observed included formally assigned and recognized tasks such as supervising custodial staff, managing substitute teacher assignments, and handling discipline, as well as such informal and self-defined tasks as making sure a lonely kid has one short conversation with an adult that day, or dropping in on a class to comment on an interesting Civil War artifact.

Widened perspectives, verification, and triangulation are important for developing a full picture of the assistant principal.

In most instances, the observations were supplemented with formal interviews with the principal, a close colleague (usually a fellow assistant principal, guidance counselor, and/or a teacher), the AP him/herself, and, where possible, the AP's spouse. The formal interviewing was designed to obtain essential background data, but also to be open-ended, encouraging the assistants to shape their responses in accordance with how they saw their lives. (See the interview protocols in Appendix C.)

## Step 3: Open-Ended Surveys

*(Incorporating 26 people)*

A survey was devised to expand the data collection and to provide a method for verifying the findings from the observation and interviewing. Twenty-six usable responses to the 93 mailed surveys provided the needed expansion and verification. Respondents represented 22 states and the District of Columbia. Every region of the country—midwest, upper northwest, west, New England, mid-Atlantic—was represented. School districts ranged from one rural area that encompassed 170 square miles, to cities the size of Anchorage and Little Rock.

Some interesting details about these respondents:

- They had served under 1 to 10 principals.
- Their age range was 40 to 62 years (average age: 49).

➤ Three of the 26 had earned a doctorate.

➤ Their number of years in administration ranged from 7 to 29 (average: 15).

➤ The sample included 7 women and 19 men.

This multi-method research aimed to collect data capturing a portrait of the inner lives and daily routines of career assistant principals. It also expanded and verified findings through a wide sample, incorporating data from 50 APs in a wide range of settings and with varied backgrounds.

# Appendix B
# Focus Group Interview Guide

## Thematic Statements

▶ Being an assistant principal has many rewards and satisfactions.

▶ Most people fail to see the vital role assistants play in schools.

▶ There are particular elements in my work and life arrangements that make my assistantship more satisfying than you would expect.

▶ There are particular elements in my work and life arrangements that make my assistantship awfully difficult—that undermine my satisfaction.

▶ Anyone trying to capture the essence of the assistant principalship should not fail to look at this.

# Appendix C
## Open-Ended Survey

### Career Assistant Principal Worksheet

*Information about you, your school district, and your job will help us to create a composite sketch of the career assistant principal. Will you please take a moment to fill out this sheet, then return it to me in the stamped envelope I've provided. All information provided will be confidential. Thank you so much for your help.*

**Personal Profile**

Name/Mailing Address: _____
                         *(optional)*

Your age: ____ Gender: ____ Race: ____ State where employed: ____

Age when you first entered administration: ____

# years in current position: ____

Highest degree, major and
granting institution: _____

Professional associations
to which you belong: _____

_____

Previous positions in education: _____

_____

Other career pursuits (before, during, or planned for after education career):

_____

_____

Number of principals you've worked under as assistant: ____

**Institutional Profile**

# of students enrolled in your school, Spring 1992: _____

Grades served: _____

Demographic description of your school: # of children on free lunch; percent minority; percent considered "at risk," etc. Please note factors that distinguish your school from others.

_____

_____

Location: (urban, suburban, rural—size of service area both in terms of population and square miles) _____

State certification requirements for assistant principal and principal:

_____

**Job Profile**

*(Please feel free to use the reverse side of this paper or another sheet if you need more space.)*

1. The thing I value most about my job is . . .

2. I wouldn't have become an assistant principal except . . .

3. The things that help me most, day to day, are . . .

4. The things that help me most, over the long haul, are . . .

5. I might well have left my position a long time ago were it not for . . .

6. The best thing the school district, or principal, or superintendent [speak to one or all, but please specify your subject] ever did for assistant principals was . . .

7. The _____ (university, professional association, state department of education, teacher's union—you fill in the blank) have done good things for assistant principals, too. For example,

8. There are certain people, often unrecognized, who make my work easier and more satisfying. They are:_____
*(identify by position)*

They make my work life more pleasant by . . .

# References

Austin, D.B., and Brown, H.L., Jr. *Report on the Assistant Principalship: Volume 3*. Reston, Va.: National Association of Secondary School Principals, 1970.

Bogdan, S., and Biklen, R. *Qualitative Research for Education*. Boston: Allyn and Bacon, 1992.

Helgesen, S. *The Female Advantage: Women's Ways of Leadership*. New York: Doubleday Currency, 1990.

Marshall, C. *The Assistant Principal: Leadership Choices and Challenges*. Newbury Park, Calif.: Corwin Press, 1992.

Marshall, C; Mitchell, B.A.; Gross, R.; and Scott, D. "The Assistant Principalship: A Career Position or a Stepping-Stone to the Principalship?" *NASSP Bulletin*, January 1992, pp. 80-88.